Step Aerobics & Aerobic Dance

An Integrated Life of Fitness

Core Workouts

Cross-Training

Eating Right & Additional Supplements for Fitness

Endurance & Cardio Training

Exercise for Physical & Mental Health

Flexibility & Agility

Sports & Fitness

Step Aerobics & Aerobic Dance

Weightlifting & Strength Building

Yoga & Pilates

An Integrated
Life of Fitness

Step Aerobics &
Aerobic Dance

SARA JAMES

Mason Crest

Mason Crest
450 Parkway Drive, Suite D
Broomall, PA 19008
www.masoncrest.com

Printed and bound in the United States of America.

First printing
9 8 7 6 5 4 3 2 1

Series ISBN: 978-1-4222-3156-2
Hardcover ISBN: 978-1-4222-3164-7
Paperback ISBN: 978-1-4222-3202-6
ebook ISBN: 978-1-4222-8702-6

Cataloging-in-Publication Data on file with the Library of Congress.

CONTENTS

KEY ICONS TO LOOK FOR:

Text-Dependent Questions: These questions send the reader back to the text for more careful attention to the evidence presented there.

Words to Understand: These words with their easy-to-understand definitions will increase the reader's understanding of the text, while building vocabulary skills.

Series Glossary of Key Terms: This back-of-the book glossary contains terminology used throughout this series. Words found here increase the reader's ability to read and comprehend higher-level books and articles in this field.

Research Projects: Readers are pointed toward areas of further inquiry connected to each chapter. Suggestions are provided for projects that encourage deeper research and analysis.

Sidebars: This boxed material within the main text allows readers to build knowledge, gain insights, explore possibilities, and broaden their perspectives by weaving together additional information to provide realistic and holistic perspectives.

INTRODUCTION

Choosing fitness as a priority in your life is one of the smartest decisions you can make! This series of books will give you the tools you need to understand how your decisions about eating, sleeping, and physical activity can affect your health now and in the future.

And speaking of the future: YOU are the future of our world. We who are older are depending on you to build something wonderful— and we, as lifelong advocates of good nutrition and physical activity, want the best for you throughout your whole life.

Our hope in these books is to support and guide you to instill healthy behaviors beginning today. You are in a unique position to adopt healthy habits that will guide you toward better health right now and avoid health-related problems as an adult.

You have the power of choice today. We recognize that it's a very busy world filled with overwhelming choices that sometimes get in the way of you making wise decisions when choosing food or in being active. But no previous training or skills are needed to put this material into practice right away.

We want you to have fun and build your confidence as you read these books. Your self-esteem will increase. LEARN, EXPLORE, and DIS-COVER, using the books as your very own personal guide. A tremendous amount of research over the past thirty years has proven that the quality of your health and life will depend on the decisions you make today that affect your body, mind, and inner self.

You are an individual, liking different foods, doing different things, having different interests, and growing up in different families. But you are not alone as you face these vital decisions in your life. Those of us in the fitness professions are working hard to get healthier foods into your schools; to make sure you have an opportunity to be physically active on a regular basis; to ensure that walking and biking are encouraged in your communities; and to build communities where healthy, affordable foods can be purchased close to home. We're doing all we can to support you. We've got your back!

Moving step by step to healthier eating habits and increasing physical activity requires change. Change happens in small steps, so be patient with yourself. Change takes time. But get started *now*.

Lead an "action-packed" life! Your whole body will thank you by becoming stronger and healthier. You can look and do your best. You'll feel good. You'll have more energy. You'll reap the benefits of smart lifestyle choices for a healthier future so you can achieve what's important to you.

Choose to become the best you can be!

—Diana H. Hart, President
National Association for Health and Fitness

Words to Understand

dedication: The quality of being devoted to doing something.

motivation: The reason that you do something, or excitement that you feel about doing something.

evolved: Changed over time.

resilience: The ability to recover quickly or bounce back.

ligaments: Tough, stretchy bands that connect bones together.

investors: People who put money into a new business, hoping that the business will make them more money in the future.

rehabilitative: Helping someone to recover after an injury or illness.

catering: Meeting a certain type of person's needs.

routines: Fixed programs or sequences of actions you follow in order.

Chapter One

WHAT ARE STEP AEROBICS AND AEROBIC DANCE?

Exercising is an important part of staying healthy. However, staying in shape requires a lot of hard work and **dedication**. Exercise experts and professional trainers recommend exercising at least least thirty minutes per day for three to four days out of a week. One of the largest hurdles people face while following an exercise routine is finding the **motivation** to start exercising and sticking with it.

Many different forms of exercise have been built around the idea that exercising should be about having fun in addition to getting in

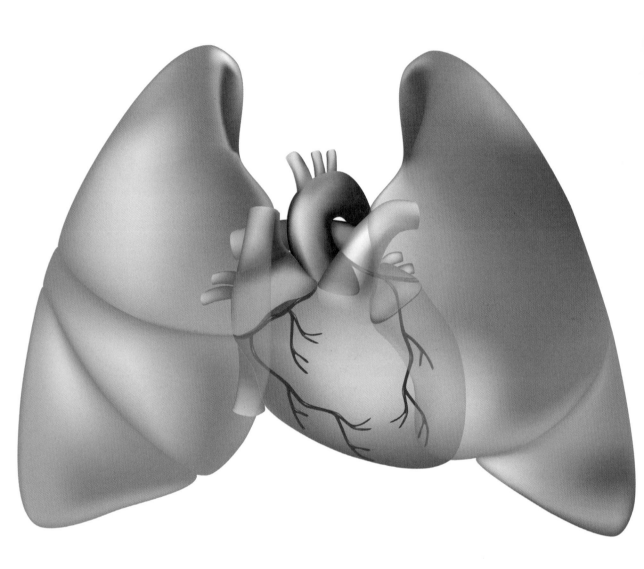

The heart and the lungs are also made up of muscles. The more you exercise, the stronger they get and the better they work—and the better your lungs and heart work, the longer your body can keep exercising.

Step Aerobics & Aerobic Dance

shape. Step aerobics and aerobic dance are two examples of exercises created for this very purpose. They were intended to make people feel excited about exercising on a regular basis. This approach to exercise has caused step aerobics and aerobic dance to become very successful.

AEROBIC EXERCISE

Exercising has **evolved** a lot over the years. Every exercise had different benefits, and people were slowly figuring out what they were. Medical researchers discovered that forcing the body as a whole to work longer and harder than it usually does increases the **resilience** of the cardiovascular system (your heart and blood vessels). The heart and lungs are strengthened during cardiovascular exercise, leading to a decreased risk of heart disease.

Dr. Kenneth Cooper was one of the many people who understood the importance of strengthening the heart and lungs through repeated exercise. He created the term "aerobics" in 1963, and he even wrote a book about its many benefits. Over thirty million copies of that book have been sold, causing it to become one of the most popular books about the importance of physical fitness. Since then, plenty of aerobic exercises have been created and refined over the years.

Running, bicycling, and swimming are among the most basic of

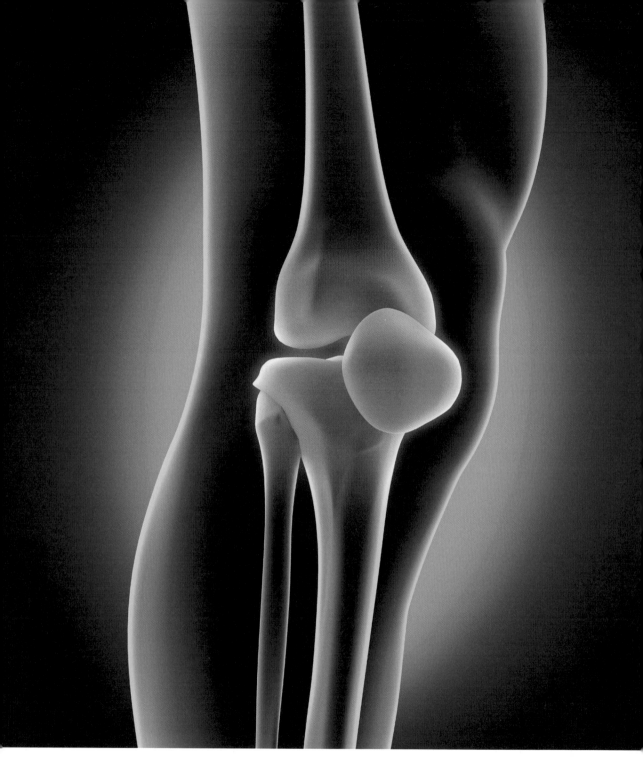

The joints in your knees get a lot of use, which can lead to injuries. Step aerobics are a good way to gradually get joints back in shape.

Step Aerobics & Aerobic Dance

aerobic exercises, but they didn't appeal to everyone. Some people wanted to exercise, but they found it boring to do the same thing over and over again. They wanted exercise to be more fun and interesting than it currently was. Fortunately, step aerobics and aerobic dance came along to fill that void. Both forms of exercise have surged in popularity since their creation.

THE BEGINNING OF STEP AEROBICS

Step aerobics as they are known today can be traced back to Gin Miller, who first introduced this form of exercise around 1989. Gin Miller loved sports as she was growing up, and she performed as a gymnast in college. While training very hard, she suffered an overuse injury to her knee. Overuse injuries occur when muscles, *ligaments*, and joints are used more often than they should be and become worn down and weak as a result. This type of injury is very common in gymnasts who train for hours each day, even if the gymnasts are very careful.

Gin sought the help of an orthopedic doctor to help her strengthen her knee again. Her doctor suggested that she ease her knee back into gymnastics by stepping on and off a milk crate repeatedly. Gin went home and, determined to make her knee better, followed her doctor's orders. She loved being outdoors, so she used her front porch for stepping instead of a milk crate.

The exercises were helping, but they weren't very fun. Gin was bored of doing the same steps over and over again. One of the ways she fixed her feelings of boredom was by listening to upbeat music while doing her step exercises. The fast-paced music made her routine fun, and she began looking forward to exercising each day.

Gin was eager to share what she had created with the local gym she taught at, and she decided to start her own classes. Gold's Gym accommodated the classes by building a large wooden bench in the exercise room that people could use to step up and down. The classes filled very quickly, making the one large bench extremely crowded and uncomfortable for everyone to use. To make more space, this large bench was cut into smaller pieces and placed throughout the room.

The steps used in step aerobics are light enough to be convenient and portable.

Step Aerobics & Aerobic Dance

The steps used during step aerobics are usually made out of plastic so that they are easy to carry around and move. Small pieces can be attached underneath both sides of the step to make the step taller or shorter. Being able to adjust the height allows people to use the step for different purposes.

These smaller boxes made it easier for people to step up and down without being too close to another person.

Investors caught wind of Gin's great idea, and the first official step for step aerobics was born. This step was created and sold by The Step Company. Reebok, a shoe company, also found out about Gin's idea and hired her to create the "Step Reebok" program. Reebok paid Gin and her team to fly around the world and teach step aerobics to fitness professionals, who would then teach her form of exercise to other people.

The program's popularity spread very quickly because of its many benefits. Researchers at several universities spent time studying the program and eventually concluded that the height of the step greatly affected the energy needed to step onto it, which made the step great for *rehabilitative* therapy. People with injured knees, like Gin once had, could start off with a short step and eventually move up to a taller one.

STEP ROUTINES

Step aerobics have evolved far beyond merely stepping up and down off of a plastic step. There are many different ways to use the step, with each one *catering* to a different physical need. Changing steps every few minutes, in addition to listening to upbeat music, prevents this form of exercise from getting boring or too repetitive. Two of the most basic steps are listed below:

The most basic steps involve simply stepping on and off the step.

Step Aerobics & Aerobic Dance

- Right basic step: start behind the step, and then step up with your right foot, followed by your left. Both feet should be relatively close together. Once you are on the step, step back off with your right foot and then your left so that you are on the ground behind the step again.
- Left basic step: this is the opposite of the right basic step. Start by stepping up with your left foot. Then, step up with your right foot so both feet are on the step. Step down with your left foot first, followed by your right.

The right basic step and left basic step are often used in combination with one another, alternating the right and the left step quickly. There are several variations of these two basic steps. One example of a variation of the basic step is the v-step:

- Right v-step: start behind the step, and then step up with your right foot. Your right foot should be close to the right side of the step. Then, step up with your left foot, placing it close to the left side of the step. Your legs should be spread apart. When you step down, start with your right foot first and end with both feet together. This movement creates a V shape!
- Left v-step: this step is the opposite of the right v-step, and should start with the left foot stepping up. Remember that while on the step, your legs should be far apart. When you step down with your left foot first followed by your right, make sure your feet are close together, creating a V.

Both the basic step and the v-step require the person exercising to start behind the step and only involve moving forward onto the step and back to step off. However, the step can be used in many ways! The turn step exercises the hips because of the way the feet must move to perform this exercise.

- Right turn step: start on the left side of the step, making sure that

The high knee step gives your thigh muscles an added workout.

Step Aerobics & Aerobic Dance

the step is lengthwise next to you. Step up with your right foot first, followed by your left. Your feet should be positioned on the step the same way they are when performing a basic step or v-step, except you will have needed to turn ninety degrees to be positioned this way, requiring the hips to turn. Then, step down with your right foot followed by your left. This will cause you to turn ninety degrees to your right as you step off the step. You should be next to the step, with your left side closest to it.

- Left turn step: this step is a continuation of the right turn step, and should begin with you on the right side of the step. Step up onto the platform with your left foot, followed by your right. Step off with your left foot, turning your body ninety degrees to your left. You will now be on the left side of the platform, where you began before starting the right turn step.

The turn step is not the only type of step move that can be done starting on the right or left side of the step. The step over is a simple way to move from one side of the platform to the other without needing to turn.

- Right step over: start on the left side of the step so that it is facing lengthwise. Step up using your right foot, followed by your left. Step down off of the step to the right side of it with your right foot first, followed by your left.

The better you get at step aerobics, the more you'll be able to add challenging variations to your routines.

Step Aerobics & Aerobic Dance

- Left step over: start on the right side of the step, repeating the steps used in the right step over except leading with the left foot first.

The most basic step *routines* only involve stepping, but there are several variations of steps that require the legs, knees, and even arms to move more than in the basic steps. The following step is a variation of the right and left basic step:

- Right high knee step: start behind the step as though you were going to perform a basic step or v-step. Step up onto the step using your right foot. As you bring your left foot up, do not place it down next to the right foot on the step. Instead, lift it up close to your chest so that it is bent. Then, place the left knee back on the ground behind the step, and step off with the right foot.
- Left high knee step: this step is identical to the right high knee step except it begins with the left foot stepping up, followed by the right knee being bent above the step. Step down onto the ground with the right foot first, followed by the left.

As you become more physically fit, you can add even more variations to basic step routines. Moving the arms while performing different step routines will increase the level of cardiovascular endurance being achieved. The best way to learn each step is to watch someone doing it by either attending a class at a local gym or watching a video of someone showing how to perform different step routines.

AEROBIC DANCE

Like step aerobics, aerobic dance was created as a fun way to stay in shape while having fun at the same time. It combines music, dance, and exercise moves to get the body in shape while also keeping people from getting bored. Aerobic dance cannot be traced back to any one person because many people began combining music and dance moves as a form of exercise at the same time.

Jazzercise is now a franchise, which means that there's a chain of many Jazzercise studios. In fact, in 2011, it was the number-one exercise franchise. Today, Jazzercise involves 7,800 instructors teaching more than 32,000 classes weekly in all American states, as well as thirty-two countries.

Text-Dependent Questions

1. Who first created the term "aerobics" and what does the term mean?
2. When and why did Gin Miller come up with the idea for step aerobics?
3. What happened as a result of Reebok hiring Gin Miller?
4. Which of the five step routines work out the hips the most? Explain.
5. How can lifting the knees or moving the arms make a step workout more effective?
6. How does the music used during aerobic dance affect the intensity of the workout?

One of the first known forms of aerobic dance was Jazzercise, where dancers were encouraged to follow the moves of an instructor who combined both dance and exercise as the dancers moved around the room listening to music. While Jazzercise began in the 1969, it wasn't until the 1970s that a combination of dance and exercise truly became popular as many different aerobic classes started using dance as a form of exercise.

Aerobic dance is as diverse as the music that is used during an aerobic dance class. Country dancing is just one example of a type of aerobic dance that started after aerobic dance grew in popularity. Today, aerobic dancers have many different genres to choose from. Some dance forms are very upbeat, while others are slow and relaxing. A person recovering from an injury might attend a slower class, while people looking to get in shape might attend a faster-paced one. Some aerobic dancers choose a certain type of dance style simply because they like the music.

But they all have one thing in common—they're great ways to get fit!

Words to Understand

endurance: The ability to keep going for a long time.

effective: Good at something; causing the intended result.

diabetes: A disease where your body can't use sugar to make energy correctly.

metabolism: All of the body's chemical reactions.

Chapter Two

THE FITNESS BENEFITS OF STEP AEROBICS AND AEROBIC DANCE

S tep aerobics and aerobic dance are designed to be so fun that you forget they were originally created to be forms of exercise— but these are serious exercises, with many physical benefits.

The best way to achieve the maximum health benefits of exercising is by following some sort of exercise plan. People who teach step aerobics and aerobic dance will be able to show you exactly which exercises should be performed to work out every area of the body. If you cannot take a class, ordering a DVD or watching a video online are

Runners don't only use their leg muscles. They also need good hearts and lungs in order to be able to keep running for long periods of time.

Step Aerobics & Aerobic Dance

two other options. The most effective programs will explain which physical benefits each step is working toward before that step is performed.

THE FIVE COMPONENTS OF PHYSICAL FITNESS

Every exercise serves a different purpose. For example, running will make both your leg muscles and your heart strong. Weight lifting will build muscles more than running does, but it won't give your heart a workout. Neither exercise will address all aspects of physical fitness, so you need to use a combination of exercises to work toward a well-rounded and healthy body.

The different aspects of physical fitness are separated into five categories known as the components of physical fitness. They are: cardiovascular *endurance*, muscle endurance, muscle strength, body composition, and flexibility. Both step aerobics and aerobic dance address multiple areas of physical fitness, but neither of these forms of exercise will address all components.

Cardiovascular Endurance

Cardiovascular endurance is strengthened through aerobic exercises such as running, swimming, and bicycling. Extra oxygen is required to keep the muscles going strong for an extended period of time. Repeated cardiovascular exercise will make the heart and lungs stronger. This allows athletes to keep moving for a very long time without needing to stop or rest.

Muscle Endurance and Muscle Strength

Muscle endurance and muscle strength are two very important components of physical fitness, but they are worked out in different ways. Muscle endurance can increase with aerobic activity if it involves a lot of body movement. Leg muscles will gain more endurance from running, while arm muscles will gain more endurance from swimming. These muscles will be able to work for an extended period of time without becoming tired due to their increased muscular endurance.

Doing warm-up exercises like this before you do aerobic exercise helps prevent injuries and also builds flexibility.

Step Aerobics & Aerobic Dance

Muscle strength is different from muscle endurance in that it is not measured by the amount of time a muscle can keep working, but rather by how much weight that muscle can lift at one time. Weight lifting is a good example of an exercise that will increase muscle strength. Push-ups, sit-ups, and pull-ups are all good ways to increase both muscle strength and endurance.

Body Composition

The human body is made up of many different components. Organs, fat, and muscle are just a few of these components. While the body should always contain some fat, it should never contain an excess amount. The ratio of muscle to fat found in the body is known as body composition. A combination of eating healthy food, getting enough sleep, and using the right exercises will help athletes achieve and maintain a good body composition.

Flexibility

Flexibility is the final component of physical fitness. Warm-up and cool-down exercises will help keep the body flexible, while at the same time preventing injury. Flexible bodies will have an easier time performing new exercises as well. Exercises like gymnastics, yoga, and Pilates all improve flexibility.

STEP AEROBICS, AEROBIC DANCE, & CARDIOVASCULAR ENDURANCE

Aerobic exercises focus mainly on cardiovascular endurance, and both step aerobics and aerobic dance are included in the aerobic category. These exercises require the body to move repeatedly for a continued stretch of time. They include a lot of motions that are like jogging and running, as well as many other movements that strengthen cardiovascular endurance.

People with a lot of cardiovascular endurance are said to have more

Aerobic dance is a lot of fun, but it's also an excellent workout for your heart and lungs. Moving your legs and arms to the beat of music will get your heart and lungs working hard too.

30 Step Aerobics & Aerobic Dance

Make Connections: Choreography

 One of the ways step aerobics and aerobic dance instructors ensure that all areas of the body are being exercised equally is by creating a routine. In step aerobics, this routine might include a set of several different steps being performed in sequence to a specific song. One step might work out knee strength, while another will work out hip flexibility. An instructor will usually shout out what step to perform and when. Counting out loud makes keeping track of each step easier. These steps can be repeated several times before starting a new sequence or routine. Doing multiple steps in sequence rather than one step over and over again will prevent overuse injury.

stamina. In other words, they can move for a long period of time without getting tired or needing to stop. Most step and aerobic dance classes last anywhere from thirty minutes to an hour, providing a healthy cardiovascular workout. This workout should be repeated several times a week, either at the gym or at home, depending on what is available.

STEP AEROBICS, AEROBIC DANCE, & STRENGTHENING MUSCLES

Aerobic exercises are very *effective* at increasing muscle endurance. Muscles also naturally get stronger as they are used. Leg muscles in particular will become very strong through repeated stepping onto a step during step aerobics. Steps can be adjusted to be taller to increase the intensity of the workout. Leg strength will increase at a faster rate

Although step aerobics doesn't typically involve working out with weights, many instructors will add hand weights to the routine as a way to build upper-body muscle strength while giving the legs a workout.

when using a taller step because the legs will be required to work harder than when stepping onto a short step.

Muscles will only get so strong by performing aerobic exercises alone, though. Step aerobics and aerobic dance do not require athletes to use any parts of their body to lift anything while exercising, so the only muscle strength that will be gained through aerobics will be limited. Even the legs will not become as strong as they could become through stepping alone.

It is important to aim for a well-rounded body, so people who focus mainly on aerobic exercises should supplement themselves with muscle-strengthening exercises. Core workouts, such as pushups, sit-ups, and pull-ups will make the muscles stronger than simple movement, but lifting weights is the best way to dramatically increase muscle strength. Athletes should ease into weight lifting slowly, and only lift as much weight as they can handle before moving on to a more intense session.

STEP AEROBICS, AEROBIC DANCE, & LOSING WEIGHT

One of the greatest benefits of aerobic exercise is that it can help participants lose weight and improve their body composition. This begins with the burning of calories.

Calories are a measurement of energy; one calorie is equal to the amount of energy required to raise the temperature of one gram of water by one degree Celsius. When we talk about calories in relation to food, we're really talking about how much energy that food will give our bodies. What our bodies don't use up, they store—which is why too many calories can end up making us fat.

Exercises performed at a faster pace will burn calories at a faster rate, and the longer we exercise, the more calories we burn. An exercise that lasts for less than thirty minutes is not as effective at burning fat, though, because that is not enough time for the body to start using excess, stored fat. Instead, it will probably use energy from the food we ate most recently.

Having a leaner body has lots of benefits that are actually more

Exercise is an important part of any healthy weight-loss plan.

Step Aerobics & Aerobic Dance

Research Project

Many different routines are included in step aerobics and aerobic dance. Each one affects the body in a different way. Using the Internet, research three steps that haven't been included in this book. Explain what the benefits of each step are and why they are an important part of a routine. What elements of fitness do these step build? Which fitness elements are left out?

important than appearance. People with a good body composition can avoid preventable problems such as *diabetes*, heart disease, and joint issues. People who have a lot of excess fat will have more trouble moving around, thus putting more pressure on the bones that must support the extra fat. Bodies with a lot of muscle will feel less strain and be able to move easier. A lean body is also more likely to have a better *metabolism*.

STEP AEROBICS, AEROBIC DANCE, AGILITY, & FLEXIBILITY

The speed at which a person can change body positions is known as agility. Quickly switching from one step routine to another during step aerobics builds agility. Aerobic dance also includes a lot of different moves that require fast movement and position changes. The faster the music, the more agility required.

Agility has a lot of benefits outside of exercise routines. Being able to react quickly to an emergency or sprinting at a moment's notice are just two reasons to improve your agility. Step aerobics and aerobic dance are also great ways to prepare for playing team sports, which often require a lot of agility.

Step aerobics or aerobic dance could help you build the agility and flexibility you need for a sport like soccer.

Joints that are allowed to stay still for too long could lead to pain and stiffness, so it is important to move every part of the body frequently. Flexibility is trained naturally through certain aerobic exercises.

Step Aerobics & Aerobic Dance

Lifting up the knee while performing a high knee step not only increases strength, but it also helps the knee bend more easily. Moving the arms from left to right while swinging the hips during a dance routine will increase hip and shoulder flexibility.

Building fitness is a good reason to get involved with step aerobics and aerobic dance. But these forms of exercise have other benefits as well!

Chapter Three

OTHER HEALTH BENEFITS OF STEP AEROBICS AND AEROBIC DANCE

Step aerobics and aerobic dance have plenty of physical fitness, but they also have some mental and social benefits.

MENTAL BENEFITS

Sleeping well is an important part of staying healthy, and active adults should aim for at least eight hours of uninterrupted sleep each night. Fortunately, regular exercise can help you achieve this goal. Research

A good night's sleep is an important part of feeling good, both emotionally and physically.

Step Aerobics & Aerobic Dance

Make Connections: Looking Good

A good step aerobics or aerobic dance routine will not only get a body in shape, but it will also make the body look good. The leg, stomach, and arm muscles of a person who exercises regularly will become very toned compared to the muscles found on people who do not work out often. Having a healthy and good-looking body can lead to a higher self-esteem, which is another mental health benefit.

has shown that people who exercise using step aerobics and aerobic dance are more likely to find it easier to fall asleep and stay asleep at the end of the day.

Getting enough sleep comes along with its own benefits. The body rests and repairs during sleep, and this is especially important if the body has experienced a lot of stress before being able to rest. Muscles that are used during intense and repeated activity require sleep to heal, and it is only during this time that the muscles are repaired. Being well rested allows these muscles to work just as hard the next day, and reduces the likelihood that they will be sore when worked out again.

Exercising itself has been linked with reducing stress and negative emotions. People who exercise regularly are less likely to have feelings of depression and anxiety. Not having to deal with anxiety caused by everyday stress will allow these people to have an easier time paying attention to school or work. They will also have more time to devote to other fun activities outside of exercise!

HAVING FUN

Step aerobics and aerobic dance have found a way to make exercising fun without sacrificing any of its health benefits. The fact that these

The bouncy beat of an aerobics class can help you keep exercising longer than if you were just doing regular exercises.

exercises are so fun may be part of the reason why they affect mental health in such a positive way!

One of the hardest parts of getting fit is sticking with a regular routine. Plenty of people who start an exercise routine will work out for a few weeks and then give up because they are tired of it, bored, or just aren't feeling the effects right away. The first few weeks of working out can lead to soreness and tiredness, so people who are just starting out may not stay motivated. If the exercise is boring, it can be even harder

Make Connections: Exercise Anywhere

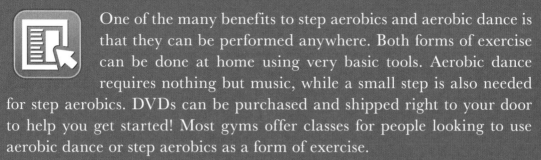

One of the many benefits to step aerobics and aerobic dance is that they can be performed anywhere. Both forms of exercise can be done at home using very basic tools. Aerobic dance requires nothing but music, while a small step is also needed for step aerobics. DVDs can be purchased and shipped right to your door to help you get started! Most gyms offer classes for people looking to use aerobic dance or step aerobics as a form of exercise.

to stay focused. People who are enjoying their exercise routines are more likely to stick with it and less likely to quit.

SOCIAL BENEFITS

Both step aerobics and aerobic dance give participants the opportunity to meet other people. Classes hosted at local gyms are often filled with dozens of diverse people who are all exercising for very different reasons. Meeting these people and making friends with them can lead to better lifestyle choices of all sorts.

Make Connections: Zumba®

Many forms of aerobic dance are inspired by different cultures. Zumba is an exercise that mixes exercise with Latin dance and Latin music. Elements of popular Latin dances, such as salsa, are a common part of Zumba dance routines.

Taking a Jazzercise or Zumba class is a great way to keep yourself motivated to exercise.

Text-Dependent Questions

1. What are two of the mental health benefits of aerobic exercise described by the author?
2. Explain why sleep is an important part of a fitness program.
3. What are reasons why a person might give up on an exercise program?
4. What are some of the benefits to having an exercise buddy?

Working out with other people has another benefit, too; people who work out in the company of others are less likely to stop working out. If you miss a day of class, your friend might ask you where you have been. That sort of social pressure could stop you from blowing off a class even when you are tempted to. Agreeing to carpool to an exercise class with a friend is also a good way to keep yourself from falling out of an exercise routine.

Step aerobics and aerobic dance actively encourage participants to work together, even when not in class. You can make a plan to exercise with a friend outside of class to stay even more fit. Staying motivated by working together is one of the greatest benefits of having a friend to exercise with. You can push each other to work harder. You can build fitness together—and have fun too!

Words to Understand

prerequisites: Requirements before you can do something.

Chapter Four

STEP AEROBICS AND AEROBIC DANCE SAFETY

Any time you exercise, there's a risk you could hurt yourself. The benefits of exercise outweigh the risks, though. The smart way to look at it is know how to stay safe while exercising. There are plenty of ways to ensure that your workout is safe, both before, during, and after a workout session.

BEFORE EXERCISE

Getting ready to exercise is just as important as exercising itself! Eating the right kind of food, drinking enough water, and getting enough sleep are three *prerequisites* for a good workout.

Water is essential to good health. You'll need even more of it than usual when you're exercising.

Step Aerobics & Aerobic Dance

A big meal full of carbohydrates and proteins will help you push through a long day of exercising. The carbohydrates—complex sugars—provide energy, while the protein fuels the muscles and repairs them after they have been exercised. Carbohydrates can be found in cereal, pasta, and rice, while proteins can be found in meat, fish, and beans. But that doesn't mean you should eat a big meal right before you exercise. It's a better idea to eat earlier in the day. Otherwise, when you try to exercise, your blood will be going to your stomach instead of your muscles.

Water is vital to good health, and you'll need even more than usual when you're exercising. The body is 50 to 75 percent water, which means that every cell in your body needs it in order to function. Your body uses water to filter the blood and remove waste. One of the ways water leaves the body is through sweat, which serves two purposes. First, it removes waste, and second, it cools down the body. As water evaporates off the skin, it reduces the temperature of the skin it evaporated from. A body that is exercising requires more water than one at rest, both because more waste needs to be removed and because the body sweats to cool itself. Always have a water bottle on hand when exercising, and make sure to drink a lot of water beforehand. Remember: if you feel thirsty, you are already slightly dehydrated!

Last, never exercise unless you have had enough sleep. The body repairs and heals during sleep, so a body that lacks sleep is more likely to become injured or fatigued. People who can normally exercise for an hour a day might feel winded after just fifteen minutes of exercise if they did not get a good night's rest.

WARM-UPS AND COOL-DOWNS

Warming up is an important part of exercise, and it must be done no matter which exercise is being performed. Aerobic exercises are no exception. Experts suggest that anyone who plans to exercise spend at least ten to fifteen minutes warming up before a thirty-minute workout session. Do not rush through the warm-ups. They're important!

Stretching is an important part of warm-ups, to get your muscles ready to work.

Step Aerobics & Aerobic Dance

Warming up reduces the likelihood of injuring yourself. Muscles tend to get stiff when they aren't being used, even if just for a day. Stiff muscles and ligaments are more likely to tear. Muscles must be slowly eased into exercise every time, no matter how experienced an athlete is. Stretching the muscles makes them warmer and increases their flexibility. They will be able stretch more and work harder too.

The first part of a good warm-up will usually stretch the legs, arms, neck and shoulders in a slow and gentle fashion. Some areas may get more attention than others because they will be worked out harder during an exercise routine. For example, step aerobics require a lot of leg movements, so legs should be warmed up more than any other part of the body.

The stretches performed during cool-downs are similar to those used in warm-ups, but they serve a slightly different purpose. As the body exercises, lactic acid is released into the muscles to help them with prolonged activity. The lactic acid can build up over time, causing pain and stiffness. Stretching before and after a workout will reduce the likelihood of lactic acid staying in the muscles. It will be able to safely spread out and will be less likely to cause pain.

Cool-downs should always begin with a lighter version of whatever exercise was being performed. Dance aerobics, for instance, should cool down with a less intense song. Participants can keep moving and dancing, but at a slower pace, giving the body time to ease out of periods of intense activity. People using step aerobics as exercise could slow down and perform steps at a slower rate, or reduce the height of the step being used. More complex steps require more energy, so cool-downs should only use the most basic of steps.

EQUIPMENT

Unlike other exercises, step aerobics and aerobic dance do not require a lot of equipment. Only a plastic step is needed for step aerobics, although a workout program to watch on television may be purchased as needed. Fortunately, aerobic steps are not very expensive. Some can be found for as little as $30, while others are more expensive because

It doesn't really matter what you wear to do either aerobic dance or step aerobics, so long as it's something comfortable that allows you to bend and move easily.

Step Aerobics & Aerobic Dance

they are sold with instructional videos. Many steps include extra pieces to adjust the height.

Wearing the right clothes and shoes are just as important as any other piece of equipment involved in aerobic exercise. Shoes that fit properly and comfortably will reduce the likelihood of your feet hurting or needing to rest while you are vigorously moving up and down on a step or across the room. Always break in your shoes before you use them to exercise, as feet that are aching will not be able to work as hard as comfortable feet.

Step aerobics and aerobic dance require a lot of movement, so clothes that accommodate that are important too. Stretch pants and a loose-fitting shirt are two good choices for workout attire. Jeans and other tight clothes will not allow you to stretch as much as you need to, and could even result in a pulled muscle if you move the wrong way.

STAYING SAFE

Many step aerobics and aerobic dance classes will only happen once a week, but that is not enough to stay in shape. Experts say that an active person should exercise at least four to five days a week, although

A physical therapist has been specially trained to help people with injuries rebuild their strength and flexibility.

Step Aerobics & Aerobic Dance

as little as three days is acceptable for people who are just starting out or recovering from an injury. This means you'll need to add some other form of exercise to your classes. You might want to do the same exercises at home, using a tape—or you might want to run or play a sport on the days when you don't have class. Be careful not to work out too often, however. One day a week should be reserved for complete and total rest. Another day should be used for flexibility exercises only.

Exercise is only truly effective if the body is ready for it. If you're sick or recovering from an illness, you aren't ready to exercise. Not only could you get your classmates sick, but you will also lack the resilience to work out as hard or as fast as you could when you were well. Pushing yourself too hard could result in injury, or make your illness even worse. It is best to take a break when you are sick and give your body the time it needs to recover.

INJURIES

Even the most athletic people can still injure themselves during a workout. It is important to stay safe—but just in case, you should also know what to do when an injury occurs. Stop working out immediately if you feel something just isn't quite right. Take time to rest, examine your body, and figure out what is wrong. A cold ice pack can be used to reduce inflammation. A doctor should always be consulted for an injury that that won't go away. There are two types of injuries: overuse injuries, and acute injuries.

An overuse injury is exactly what it sounds like: it's an injury that occurs when a muscle or ligament is used more than it should be, resulting in inflammation, soreness, or even a slight tear. Repeating the same movement over and over again is what causes an overuse injury when that particular muscle or ligament did not have proper time to rest and recover. The knee injury Gin Miller sustained that caused her to invent step aerobics was an overuse injury. As a result, step aerobics routines are very careful about avoiding overuse injuries. Plenty of different steps are included in these routines, with no single area being stressed

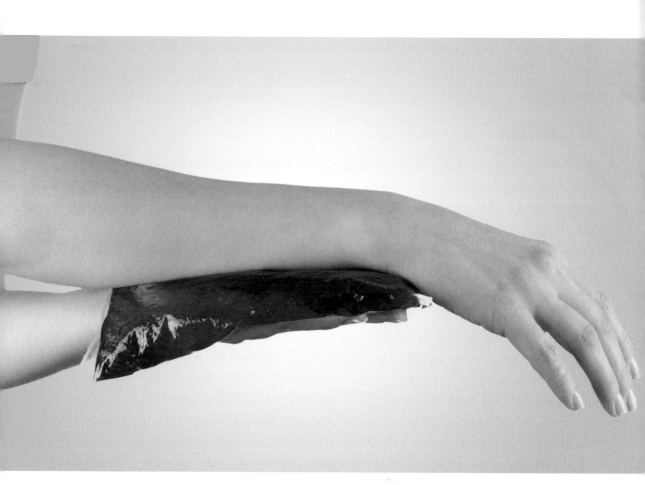

If you've injured a wrist, knee, or ankle, an ice pack will help reduce the swelling.

Text-Dependent Questions

1. Why should you drink water, eat a healthy meal, and get enough sleep before exercising? Explain.
2. Meals that are eaten before a workout should include carbohydrates and protein. What purpose do these two food groups serve?
3. What purpose do warm-ups and cool-downs serve? What might happen if you skip them?
4. What are the two types of injures and what causes them?
5. How can step aerobics help people heal and get back into exercising after they have been injured?

more than another. One step might increase knee strength, while another will work out the thighs or hips.

Acute injuries are different from overuse injuries in that they occur due to an accident or another sudden event. Falling and scraping your knee or bruising your elbow are examples of acute injuries. Always clean wounds and cover them with a bandage before returning to your exercise. More serious injuries, such as breaking a bone or hitting your head, should be brought to the attention of a medical professional.

Step aerobics can be used as a rehabilitative exercise; after all, that's what Gin Miller originally used it for! If you are working out while waiting for an injury to fully heal, remember to go slowly and for less time than before you were injured. It is best to start out with a low step as well. Always ask a doctor if it is safe to start working out again before doing it on your own. A physical therapist will be able to tell you which steps to perform to help an injury heal.

Don't let injuries discourage you. Exercise is the best way to build a strong and healthy body—so as soon as you can, get back on that floor and start moving again!

FIND OUT MORE

In Books

Brown, Lee E., and Vance Ferrigno. *Training for Speed, Agility, and Quickness.* Champaign, IL: Human Kinetics, 2005.

Lancaster, Scott B., and Radu Teodorescu. *Athletic Fitness for Kids.* Champaign, IL: Human Kinetics, 2008.

Mazzeo, Karen S. *Fitness through Aerobics, Step Training, Walking.* Belmont, CA: Cengage Learning, 2007.

Pahmeier, Iris, and Corinna Niederbäumer. *Step Aerobics: Fitness Training for Schools, Clubs and Studios.* Oxford, UK: Meyer & Meyer Sport, 2011.

Pérez, Beto, and Maggie Greenwood-Robinson. *Zumba: Ditch the Workout, Join the Party!* New York: Wellness Central, 2009.

Online

About Gin Miller
ginmillerfitness.com/defining-gin-miller

Benefits of Step Aerobics
www.superpages.com/supertips/step-aerobics-2.html

History of Aerobic Dance
www.livestrong.com/article/121986-history-aerobic-dance

Returning to Exercise After Injury
www.intelihealth.com/article/
returning-to-exercise-after-injury?hd=Focus

Understanding Aerobic
www.healthnwealth.in/aerobics.html

SERIES GLOSSARY OF KEY TERMS

abs: Short for abdominals. The muscles in the middle of your body, located over your stomach and intestines.

aerobic: A process by which energy is steadily released using oxygen. Aerobic exercise focuses on breathing and exercising for a long time.

anaerobic: When lots of energy is quickly released, without using oxygen. You can't do anaerobic exercises for a very long time.

balance: Your ability to stay steady and upright.

basal metabolic rate: How many calories your body burns naturally just by breathing and carrying out other body processes.

bodybuilding: Exercising specifically to get bigger, stronger muscles.

calories: The units of energy that your body uses. You get calories from food and you use them up when you exercise.

carbohydrates: The foods that your body gets most of its energy from. Common foods high in carbohydrates include sugars and grains.

cardiovascular system: Your heart and blood vessels.

circuit training: Rapidly switching from one exercise to another in a cycle. Circuit training helps build endurance in many different muscle groups.

circulatory system: The system of blood vessels in your body, which brings oxygen and nutrients to your cells and carries waste products away.

cool down: A gentle exercise that helps your body start to relax after a workout.

core: The muscles of your torso, including your abs and back muscles.

cross training: When an athlete trains for a sport she normally doesn't play, to exercise any muscle groups she might be weak in.

dehydration: When you don't have enough water in your body. When you exercise, you lose water by sweating, and it's important to replace it.

deltoids: The thick muscles covering your shoulder joint.

energy: The power your body needs to do things like move around and keep you alive.

endurance: The ability to keep going for a long time.

flexibility: How far you can bend, or how far your muscles can stretch.

glutes: Short for gluteals, the muscles in your buttocks.

hydration: Taking in more water to keep from getting dehydrated.

isometric: An exercise that you do without moving, by holding one position.

isotonic: An exercise you do by moving your muscles.

lactic acid: A chemical that builds up in your muscles after you exercise. It causes a burning feeling during anaerobic exercises.

lats: Short for latissimus dorsi, the large muscles along your back.

metabolism: How fast you digest food and burn energy.

muscle: The parts of your body that contract and expand to allow you to move.

nervous system: Made up of your brain, spinal cord, and nerves, which carry messages between your brain, spinal cord, and the rest of your body.

nutrition: The chemical parts of the food you eat that your body needs to survive and use energy.

obliques: The muscles to either side of your stomach, under your ribcage.

pecs: Short for pectorals, the muscles on your chest.

quads: Short for quadriceps, the large muscle on the front of your upper leg and thigh.

reps: How many times you repeat an anaerobic exercise in a row.

strength: The power of your muscles.

stretching: Pulling on your muscles to make them longer. Stretching before you exercise can keep you flexible and prevent injuries.

warm up: A light exercise you do before a workout to get your body ready for harder exercise.

weight training: Exercises that involve lifting heavy weights to increase your strength and endurance.

INDEX

ABOUT THE AUTHOR AND THE CONSULTANT

Sara James is a writer and blogger. She writes educational books for children on a variety of topics, including health, history, and current events.

Diane H. Hart, Nationally Certified Fitness Professional and Health Specialist, has designed and implemented fitness and wellness programs for more than twenty years. She is a master member of the International Association of Fitness Professionals, and a health specialist for Blue Shield of Northeastern New York, HealthNow, and Palladian Health. In 2010, Diane was elected president of the National Association for Health and Fitness (NAHF), a nonprofit organization that exists to improve the quality of life for individuals in the United States through the promotion of physical fitness, sports, and healthy lifestyles. NAHF accomplishes this work by fostering and supporting state governors and state councils and coalitions that promote and encourage regular physical activity. NAHF is also the national sponsor of Employee Health and Fitness Month, the largest global workplace health and fitness event each May. American College of Sports Medicine (ACSM) has been a strategic partner with NAHF since 2009.

PICTURE CREDITS